ANNE FRANK

D0369173

BY ANNE SCHRAFF

Development: Kent Publishing Services, Inc.

Design and Production: Signature Design Group, Inc.

SADDLEBACK EDUCATIONAL PUBLISHING

Three Watson

Irvine, CA 92618-2767

Web site: www.sdlback.com

Photo Credits: pages 8, 15, 23, Anne Frank Fonds-Basel-
Amsterdam/Getty Images

ISBN-10: 1-59905-247-4

ISBN-13: 978-1-59905-247-2

eBook: 978-1-60291-608-1

Printed in the United States of America

13 12 11 10 09   3 4 5 6 7 8 9

TABLE of CONTENTS

C H A P T E R 1

Anne Frank was a young German Jewish girl who was caught up in the violent **anti-semitism** of Germany in the 1930s and 40s. On her thirteenth birthday, she was given a diary. When she and her family went into hiding during the war, she wrote her deepest feelings in her diary. In spite of the fear and suffering she experienced, Anne held on to her belief in the goodness of people. Millions of people all over the world have read her powerful diary. They have learned the shocking story of the Holocaust.

Annelies Marie Frank was born at 7:30 a.m. on June 12, 1929. Her sister, Margot, was three years older. Anne was born in Frankfurt am Main, Germany. Anne's father, Otto Frank, served in the German army during World War I. He was a businessman when he married twenty-five-year-old Edith Hollander. He was thirty-six at the time.

Otto Frank was a gentle, soft-spoken man. Edith Frank was shy and more religious than her husband. She went to the **synagogue** and celebrated the High Holy Days of the Hebrew faith.

When Anne was very small, she loved to play in her sandbox in the family garden. She and Margot played under the trees in summer. In the winter, they went sledding in the snow. Anne had a special relationship with her father. He was the one who often tucked her in at night. He told her bedtime stories, too.

Anne's father invented an ongoing story about two girls both named Paula. Good Paula was dutiful and well behaved. Bad Paula was always up to **mischief**. Margot Frank was a good student and very dutiful, but Anne was sometimes a little rebel. But she could always depend on her father to defend her when her mother got mad at her.

In 1929 the economy of Germany was very bad. A serious **depression** was sweeping the world. In the United States' the stock market had crashed. This led to bank failures and unemployment. Things were even worse in Germany. Unemployment was widespread. **Inflation** was so bad that money became almost worthless.

Adolf Hitler, a World War I veteran and failed painter, started a political party—the Nazi Party. Hitler promised to improve conditions in Germany. He blamed the Jews for Germany's problems. There had always been anti-semitism in Germany. But Hitler pushed it up to new levels. Like many German Jews, the Franks were worried about the future.

In the summer of 1929, Otto Frank's brother-in-law opened a branch of the pectin-producing company, Opekta. The branch was opened in Amsterdam, the Netherlands. Pectin is a powdered fruit extract used to make jams and jellies. Anne's family began thinking about moving to Amsterdam, too.

In 1931 the Nazi Party was growing in Germany. Hitler was making greater threats against the Jewish people. In January 1933 Hitler was elected **chancellor** of Germany. His Nazi Storm Troopers, called Brown Shirts, marched around Berlin singing songs about

Edith, Margot and Anne Frank

spilling Jewish blood. Otto Frank decided it was time to leave Germany.

A law was passed in Germany forcing Jewish children to be taught separately from others. In April 1933 a **boycott** of all Jewish stores was announced. Many anti-Jewish laws were passed, each one a little bit tougher than the ones before it.

Otto Frank went to Amsterdam in August 1933 to set up a branch of Opekta. The branch would sell pectin to housewives. He left Anne and the family behind until he found a house. He acted very quickly. Life in Germany was getting very dangerous for Jews.

In December 1933 Anne, Margot, and their mother joined their father in Amsterdam to start a new life. They felt they were safe from the Nazis.

CHAPTER 2

The Franks new home was a large, well-lit apartment. It was on the third floor of a house at 37 Merwedeplein in Amsterdam. The house was in the river quarter of the city. It was a complex filled with new houses. There were large piles of sand everywhere, and Anne and Margot enjoyed playing in it.

The house was close to the seashore. To the delight of the daughters, the Franks often went to the beach. Many German Jews were moving into the neighborhood. They were also fleeing Hitler's Germany.

Otto Frank ran his new business. He also started a second business, Pectacon B.V., selling seasonings for meats. He hired several faithful employees. Victor Kugler, an Austrian Catholic, became his right hand man.

Hermine (Miep) Santrouschitz, an orphan girl from Austria, became the typist, bookkeeper, and public relations person. Anne's father and Miep, as she was called, became close friends.

Anne's mother was homesick for Germany. But Anne and Margot liked life in the Netherlands. They both picked up the Dutch language very quickly and made many friends. Anne's father called her a lively child who never stopped asking questions. She was curious about everything.

When visitors came to the house, Anne would bug them with questions. Margot was a quieter girl and a very good student. She took very good care of her clothing. Anne's mother often told Anne to try to become more like her sister.

When she was seven, Anne started school at the Montessori School where her sister also attended. She learned to read and write quickly, and she wrote many letters to her relatives and old friends in Frankfurt.

In the summer of 1936, several more people joined Anne's father in his business. Johannes Kleiman became the bookkeeper. A Dutch girl, Bep Voskuijl, helped Miep with her work. The next year, Miep married a young man named Jan Gies. All of Otto Frank's employees became close friends of the Frank family.

In December 1936 Anne took a trip to Switzerland with her father. There was worry all over Europe that Adolf Hitler would attack and take over nearby countries. Anne Frank's parents worried that Hitler's armies might even reach the Netherlands.

The Van Pels family, German Jewish **refugees**, joined Otto Frank's company. They also became friends with the Frank family. The family included Peter, a young man a little older than Anne.

Anne rode her bike to school every day. She had many friends. She enjoyed going to parties and visiting the nearby ice cream parlor. Most of all, she enjoyed talking.

She was often punished by her teacher for talking during lessons. Anne was interested in many things. She liked history, movie stars, Greek mythology, writing, cats, dogs, and boys. She was getting more interested in boys every day. Anne's father noticed that she was growing into a pretty young lady. He knew the boys were looking at her too. Most of all, Anne liked to laugh.

In 1938 German armies occupied Austria. In 1939 the Germans and Russians both attacked Poland and divided it up. England and France declared war on Germany. World War II had begun. The Frank family was very scared about the future.

Three waves of Jewish refugees had left Germany and come to the Netherlands. One wave came with the Franks in 1933, another in 1935, and a third in 1938. There were **ominous** stories of terrible **persecution** of the Jews in Germany. The Jews who took refuge in the Netherlands were very fearful as the German armies grew closer.

On May 10, 1940, Germany invaded Belgium, Luxembourg, and France. These countries fell quickly. The Dutch royal family and the Dutch government escaped to England. German bombs fell on Rotterdam in the Netherlands. On May 15, 1940, the Netherlands fell to Hitler.

Miep Gies became a close friend of the Frank family after they moved to Amsterdam and she started working for Otto Frank's company.

CHAPTER 3

Anne Frank and her family and friends watched in fear as the German army marched through the streets of Amsterdam. Some of the Dutch people watched in sorrow. Some who sympathized with Hitler cheered. Of the 140,000 Jews who lived in the Netherlands, sixty percent lived in Amsterdam.

The night sky was filled with the flames and smoke of bonfires. Dutch people who wanted to gain favor with the Germans were burning English books and anti-Nazi information. A rumor spread in the Jewish neighborhoods that boats waited at the harbor to take them to England. Many Jewish families grabbed whatever they could carry and ran to the harbor. No boats were there.

Dutch people who liked Hitler raced to join the new government. They wanted to be on the winning side. But in the early days of the German **occupation** nothing much changed. Anne and Margot saw German soldiers in the street. But they kept going to school. Everybody, including the Jews, kept going to work as usual. But the Jews were holding their breath, waiting for the persecution to begin.

In October 1940 a law was passed ordering all Jewish businesses to register with the new government. Otto Frank saw what was coming. He registered his businesses but used the names of his employees, Victor Kugler and Jan Gies, as owners. This way, the registration showed that the business was non-Jewish.

In December 1940 Anne's father moved his business to a new address, 263 Prinsengracht. The building was actually two buildings connected by a hallway. There was a 17th century house in the front. In the back there was an 18th century area that had a large warehouse on the ground floor and rooms upstairs. Working there were Otto Frank's faithful employees, Johannes Kleiman, Miep, Bep, Victor Kugler, and Hermann Van Pels.

A law was passed at the end of 1940 forcing all Dutch people to register with the authorities. The Germans wanted the names and addresses of all the Jews. At the same time, all known Jews who held government jobs were fired.

In 1942 all Dutch citizens were issued an identity card, which they had to carry when they left their homes. If they were stopped by police they had to show this card. A large letter J was stamped on the identity cards issued to Jews.

Harassment of Jewish people had been a fact of life at times over the centuries in Europe. For this reason, many Jews in the Netherlands put up with the annoying new laws. They hoped things would not get any worse. Many non-Jewish Dutch people ended their friendships with Jews. They were afraid of being found guilty by the new Nazi rulers for associating with the Jews.

In May 1942 all Jews age six and over were required to wear a yellow star with the word "Jew" written in the middle. In 1941 Anne Frank spent her last year at the Montessori school. A new law forced Jewish children to attend only Jewish schools. Anne and Margot had to enroll in a Jewish academy. Other new laws did not allow Jews to ride public transportation. They could be on the street shopping only between the hours of three to five o'clock. All Jews had to be indoors by eight in the evening. They had to stay there until six the next morning.

In June 1942 Anne and Margot tried to live as normal a life as was possible. They played ping-pong with their friends and bought ice cream at the one store where Jews were allowed. Anne's report card for the 1941-42 school year was very good except for a poor grade in algebra.

On the morning of June 12, 1942, Anne Frank woke up, filled with excitement. It was her thirteenth birthday. The family gathered in the living room to open presents. Anne was given books, a jigsaw puzzle, a brooch, candy, and the best gift of all—a hardcover diary with a red and white checkerboard cover.

CHAPTER 4

Anne Frank had never had a diary before. She loved it and named it "Kitty." The diary became her best friend in which she would **confide** her most secret thoughts. On the inside of the checkered cover, Anne put a photograph of herself.

On June 14, Anne began to write in her diary. She had met a new friend, sixteen-year-old Hello Silberberg. He was a good looking boy. A few days later, Hello visited Anne at home. They shared cream cakes, biscuits, and tea. Then they took a walk in the twilight. It was after eight when Anne got home. Her father was very upset. The Jewish curfew of eight o'clock was very strict. Anne told "Kitty," her diary, how much she enjoyed that day.

Anne began writing about her life in her diary.

At this time, Otto Frank no longer went to work at his factory. He wanted it to look like only a non-Jewish business, and his friends ran it.

Concentration camps had been operating in Germany since 1933 when Hitler took power. At first they were work camps, not **extermination camps**. Inmates died often. But the purpose of the camps was not to kill people. However, at the Wannsee Conference in Berlin in January 1942, the plan to destroy all the Jews of Europe was created. Adolf Eichmann was put in charge of operations. Poland was chosen to be the site of most death camps. Many were also in Germany. These camps would receive Jews destined to be killed.

In the Netherlands, the Westerbork refugee camp was fortified with barbed wire and operated by Nazi SS men. As Dutch Jews were picked up, they were sent there. Later, they were deported to one of the death camps in Poland or Germany. Most went to Poland. Every Tuesday, cattle trucks pulled up to take the people away.

The Dutch people were told that the Jews were being sent to work camps. Hardly anyone believed that. They would watch scared Jewish families going down the streets to the rail stations. In the end, only 25 percent of the Jews in the Netherlands survived.

Otto Frank decided to take his family into hiding. It was the only way to avoid the terrible deportation order.

All the Franks were registered. It was only a matter of time before one of them or all of them would get orders to report to the SS office. On July 5, 1942,

Margot Frank was ordered to report for deportation. The Franks now rushed their plans. They had to hide and do it quickly.

Anne Frank packed her most valuable things into a **satchel**. She took her beloved diary, hair curlers, handkerchiefs, school books, a comb, and some letters she treasured. The rest of the family also packed, leaving most of their possessions behind.

On Monday morning, July 6, at five in the morning, the Frank family walked away from their house at 37 Merwedeplein where they had lived for eight years. Everybody put on many pieces of clothing even though it was a hot day. It was easier to wear the clothing than carry it. Anne wore two vests, three pairs of pants, two pairs of stockings, shoes, a wooly cap, and a scarf. Since Jews were not allowed to use public transportation, they made the trip to the hiding place on foot.

Anne knew she and her family were going into hiding. But she did not know where they were going. Margot was told, but not Anne. Her parents feared she might accidentally tell someone. Anne's greatest worry as she walked from her home was that she was leaving her cat, Moortje, behind. The Franks had made plans for neighbors to care for the cat, but Anne was sorry to be leaving her pet.

It began to rain as the family walked slowly along. As they got closer to their destination, Anne Frank was surprised to recognize a familiar place—her father's workplace, 236 Prinsengracht.

CHAPTER 5

The hiding place was above the old warehouse, in a house connected to the front house. It could not be seen from the street. A small corridor led to a movable bookcase. Behind the bookcase was what was called the secret **annex**. Their new home had three bedrooms, a bathroom, and an attic where their food was stored. From the attic window you could see a large chestnut tree.

When the Franks arrived, Miep Gies quickly took them to the secret annex. When they were all inside, she quickly closed the door. The only people who knew about the hiding place were the small group of friends. They planned to supply and protect the Frank family in the days ahead. They were Miep Gies, Bep Voskuijl, Victor Kugler, and Johannes Kleiman. Bep's father found out about it later.

The plan had been carefully made. Food was **rationed** at that time in the Netherlands. For this reason, it was necessary to buy extra food for the Franks using **black market** ration cards. Bep and Miep did the shopping. They made sure to buy things in different stores. This way, they did not create suspicion. Jan Gies, Miep's husband, joined the others, and he and Kleiman got black market ration cards.

When the Franks arrived at the secret annex, they found boxes of bedding and other items to be unpacked. They worked for two days doing this. Anne and her father sewed together strips of material to make curtains for the windows so nobody could look in.

On July 13, the Van Pels family went into hiding with the Franks. This was Hermann Van Pels, his wife, Gusti, and their fifteen-year-old son, Peter. Otto Frank had worked with Hermann in the past. Peter brought his cat, Mouschi. Anne was happy with the newcomers, who made life livelier. Anne was less happy when the final member of the refugees in the secret annex arrived in November. He was Fritz Pfeffer, a family friend. He was someone who was critical of Anne's manners.

During the day when the regular

employees worked downstairs, the eight who hid upstairs had to be very quiet. The employees knew nothing about the secret annex. Everyone had to whisper when they spoke and walk lightly. Nobody could use the sink or the toilet between nine in the morning and seven in the evening.

Anne spent her days studying her schoolbooks and reading. The helpers provided books for the children. Anne learned how to write very well. The three young people, Anne, Margot, and Peter were tutored by Otto Frank. They all hoped that when the need to hide was over, they could go back to normal school and not be far behind the other students.

One of the things that made Anne sad was that she had lost contact with her friends. She also missed the freedom to go outside. Sometimes she cried herself to sleep at night. But usually Anne was her old lively self. In fact, she was so outspoken that the Van Pels complained to her mother.

Otto wanted to make the rooms where Anne and Margot lived more cheerful. He lined the walls with the girls' picture postcard collection and pictures of famous movie stars they liked. Anne wrote in her diary that the wall became one big picture.

Anne complained to her diary that Margot and Peter acted so well-behaved and old. She thought that they made her look bad by comparison. At those times, she felt lonely and friendless. She wrote in her diary to pour out her frustrations.

The eight people in the secret annex listened to the radio at night. They heard news about the war broadcast from Great Britain. They learned what was happening to Jews who had been deported. They also heard about the progress of the war. Fritz Pfeffer brought more current news too. He told the Franks and Van Pels how the Dutch Nazi authorities were going from door to door. They were asking every householder if there were any Jews in the house. Any Jew who was found, from infants to older people, was deported to the death camps.

CHAPTER 6

The routine in the secret annex became fixed. During the day, the children studied writing and languages. At night when there were no people downstairs, they listened to the news on the radio and then to classical music.

Sometimes they played board games, recited poetry, and talked about poetry. Otto Frank read aloud to the family. Religion was also a part of their lives. Anne's father was not religious. Her mother was more interested in the Jewish faith and rituals. But in the secret annex on Friday nights, they observed the **Sabbath**, led by Edith Frank and Fritz Pfeffer. They cooked Jewish foods and celebrated the High Holy Days. They even observed Christmas, not the religious aspects, but the joyful atmosphere.

Otto Frank tended to be optimistic. He even believed that this time they were spending living in the secret annex was precious because they were all close. He told his daughters that they might look back on this experience later on as a good thing.

The relationship between Anne Frank and her father had always been good, but during the hiding she grew even closer to her father. Sometimes, Anne's mother complained that Anne was not as obedient as her sister. Other times, the Van Pels or Pfeffer **criticized** her behavior. But her father always defended her. He helped Anne with her studies. She knew that whenever she was sad or depressed he would understand and comfort her. She wrote in her diary on November 7, 1942, that her father was the person she looked up to. She wrote that he was all she had in the world.

The friends who were supplying the Franks had to struggle to get food for them. They often used the black market to get canned foods. A typical supper for Anne and the others was a can of **hash** that smelled like rotten eggs.

In 1943 Anne heard planes roaring overhead. From listening to the radio broadcast from London, she knew there were Allied planes flying toward

Germany to drop their bombs. The Allied forces were a group of countries that fought against the Axis forces in World War II. The Axis forces were led by Hitler and the Germans.

The Dutch radio program broadcast from London was hopeful that these bombing raids would speed up the defeat of Germany. They hoped it would bring an end to the suffering. Anne and the others were fearful when they heard the anti-aircraft guns fire at the Allied planes from Amsterdam.

One night, the people in the secret annex heard noises from the attic where their food was stored. Peter Van Pels shone his flashlight up into the darkness. There he saw huge rats running around. From then on, Peter's cat slept in the attic.

Anne Frank enjoyed her lessons, except for algebra and geometry. She loved history above everything else. She also enjoyed writing in her diary. She also began to write a book titled *Stories and Events from the Secret Annex*. This book contained real events that had happened. It also had events created by Anne's imagination. She wrote in fine script, never sloppily.

By the end of 1943, the eight people hiding in the secret annex were worn out and weary from their long imprisonment. The food was terrible. As the war dragged on, there were worse food shortages in the Netherlands. It was harder and harder for the helpers to supply the refugees.

Anne deeply admired the people who were helping them survive. She was filled with **gratitude** at the thought that these people were risking their lives to save eight Jews. After all, they were not even related to the Franks or the others.

In July 1943 burglars entered the warehouse below the secret annex. They stole the cash box. The thieves also stole valuable food coupons. Everyone in the annex was terrified that the burglars may have seen something suspicious. They were afraid that they found out that there were people hiding upstairs.

CHAPTER 7

Nothing came of the burglary, and the refugees relaxed a little. When Anne and her family first came to the annex, her parents noted the girls' height by a mark on the kitchen wall. During the hiding, Anne had grown a full five inches. All the clothing she had brought with her did not fit anymore. Miep and Bep did their best to find some new **garments** for the girls. But, for the most part, Anne and Margot made do in their small clothing.

In September 1943 there was good news from the war front. Germany's ally, Italy, had surrendered to the Allied forces. Now only Germany and Japan remained in the war against the Allied forces. From everything the Franks were hearing from London, Germany was losing the war. But the **stubborn** Nazi armies showed no signs of an early surrender.

Anne Frank was running out of writing room in her diary. She started writing in exercise books and accounting books that Miep and Bep brought. In the fall of 1943 Anne went through a period of depression. She wrote that she felt like she was being dragged down into a bottomless darkness. She longed desperately to go outside and inhale some fresh air, but she dared not.

As 1944 began, Anne was fourteen-and-a-half-years-old. She and the others had been in hiding now for a year and a half. On a day in late February, Anne looked out the window to see the sky a glorious blue color. That lifted her spirits. She always loved to look at the big chestnut tree beyond her window. Now tiny, sparkling raindrops clung to the branches of the tree. As the tree was getting ready for spring, Anne noticed changes in her own body. She was turning from a child into a young woman. This filled her with wonder and excitement.

Anne began to notice Peter Van Pels in a different way. He was a shy young man, but he seemed to like Anne too. Anne felt as if she were falling in love with Peter. Anne looked for chances to sit beside him and look into his blue eyes. They sat beside each other on wooden crates, their arms around each other's shoulders. Birds sang outside in the chestnut tree. Anne was filled with excitement, confusion, and longing.

Sometimes, Anne told her mother how frustrated and miserable she felt. Her mother said she should think of people even worse off than they were. They were the Jews who had been rounded up and deported. But this only made Anne angry. She thought she already felt terrible, so how would focusing on the misery of others improve her depression?

In March 1944 Anne had what she described as the most wonderful evening ever in the secret annex. She and Peter opened their hearts to one another. They were standing side by side in the darkness looking out the open window. There, the shy Peter found it easier to talk. They shared their dreams for the future and their affection for one another.

There were moments of fear in the secret annex. Sometimes, some of the workers in the warehouse asked questions. They did not know that the Frank family was hiding there. They asked why Miep and Bep were always carrying food upstairs. The curious workers were told it was being stored for the future there.

On Wednesday, March 29, 1944, Anne was listening to the Dutch radio broadcast from London. She heard that after the war, all diaries and letters would be collected. Some would be published as eyewitness histories of the war. Anne was very excited. She had that wonderful diary and many loose pages as well. She wondered if her writings might be chosen for publication.

Anne had now decided she would be a writer or a journalist after the war ended and the family was free again. Anne wrote in her diary that her greatest wish in the world was to be a published writer. She even chose the title for her published diary—*Het Achterhuis (The Secret Annex).*

In April 1946, one year after her death, Anne Frank's diary was first published. Anne's dream of becoming a writer had come true.

CHAPTER 8

On April 15, 1944, Anne Frank received her first kiss from a boy. Peter kissed her through her dark hair. She noted in her diary that half of his kiss landed on her left cheek and half on her ear. Anne thought about the kiss over and over. She found it thrilling and wonderful.

Anne now seriously believed her diary would be published when the war ended. She began rewriting it and doing some editing. She got thin tracing sheets from the office below. She carefully did a second draft of her diary. But, Peter and his kiss remained foremost on her mind. Her feelings for Peter were very strong. She told her father about them. Her father told her to be careful because she was very young.

On June 6, 1944, the Allied forces landed at Normandy in the invasion named D-Day. Anne and the others in the annex were excited to hear about it. It seemed that their ordeal would soon be over. In fact, the southern part of the Netherlands was already liberated. The northern part still remained under Nazi occupation.

On June 12, 1944, six days after the Normandy invasion, Anne Frank turned 15. She and her family had been in hiding now for almost two years.

Anne Frank wrote in her diary about how terrible she thought war was. She wondered on the pages of her diary why people could not live peacefully together. She felt optimistic about the future and about her relationship with Peter Van Pels. She wrote that she loved him and he loved her. Anne believed that liberation was near. Yet, she wondered if that was too wonderful to be true. After living for so long in the secret annex, freedom seemed like a fairy tale.

Anne's feelings for Peter had their ups and downs. Sometimes she was disappointed in him because he did not talk very much. Anne felt confused. She wrote in her diary that it was so hard to be young and unsure of yourself under such terrible circumstances. She wrote about what she believed in and the high ideal she held. On July 15, 1944, Anne Frank wrote that in spite of all the misery, death, and destruction, she still believed in the goodness of the human heart.

Anne Frank wrote in her diary for the last time on August 1, 1944. She wrote how it troubled her that people did not really know her. They thought she was light and shallow because they did not know her better, deeper self.

On August 4, the weather was very hot and life was going on as usual in the secret annex. Anne's father, Otto Frank was about to give Peter a lesson in English. It was ten-thirty. When Otto Frank entered the boy's room, they both heard scary noises from downstairs.

They heard the voices of strangers. The men sounded angry and hostile.

Otto Frank and Peter shared a look of terror. The secret annex had been **betrayed**.

Five men burst into the office building. One of them was a German police officer, Karl Silberbauer. The other four men were Dutch Nazis in **civilian** clothing. They first came upon Miep, Bep, Johannes Kleiman, and Victor Kugler who were all in the office.

The five Nazis knew all about the eight people who hid upstairs. Whoever had betrayed them told the entire story. It was no use for the four helpers to deny everything.

Victor Kugler was ordered to take them upstairs and roll the bookcase aside. The five men drew their revolvers in preparation as the door to the secret annex was opened.

The Franks, Van Pelses and Pfeffer were all taken downstairs with their hands in the air. The Nazis walked behind them with their drawn pistols. Karl Silberbauer demanded to know where the valuables were kept. He took a small amount of money and jewelry, then he dumped Anne's briefcase onto the floor. Her diary and the loose pages sprayed across the floor.

One of the Nazis stared at a gray foot locker belonging to Otto Frank. It was a World War I soldier's uniform. It had been used by Lt. Otto Frank of the German army.

The eight from the secret annex and their helpers were questioned. Finally, Victor Kugler and Johannes Kleiman were arrested with those who had been hiding. The ten prisoners were loaded into a windowless police truck. They were driven from 263 Prinsengracht to a former school now used by the Nazis.

The eight spent the night in basement cells. The following day, they were all taken to a regular prison on the Weteringschans in the center of the city. For ten days, Anne and the others lived in crowded, filthy conditions. Witnesses who noticed the Franks described a very worried Otto Frank and his nervous wife. Anne and Margot wore backpacks.

The next stop was Westerbork, eighty miles from Amsterdam. The Franks traveled in a regular train but the doors were bolted shut. Otto Frank still had hope. Perhaps, he thought, he and his family would remain at Westerbork. Maybe they would not be deported to the death camps of Poland.

The Franks were registered at the camp. They all showed quiet dignity. The Franks were assigned to the punishment block. There they were forced to wear uniforms and clogs. Because they had not turned themselves in and had to be captured in hiding, they were treated worse. Otto Frank had his head shaved. Edith and the girls had their hair cut painfully short. At the punishment block, there was less food, and the work was harder.

Otto Frank was assigned to the battery shed where old batteries were chopped up. It was difficult, dirty work. Anne's father tried to save Anne from this work. He got her a job helping another woman cleaning toilets. The men and women slept in different barracks. But once, when Anne was sick, her father came to stand beside her bed for hours telling her stories.

Anne and Margot clung together during their time at Westerbork. Everybody hoped against hope that they would not be deported to the death camps. But on September 2, 1944, the names were announced for the next deportation. The Franks, the Van Pelses, and Pfeffer were included.

For three days and two nights, the

train from Westerbork traveled through the Netherlands, Germany, and Poland. The people were held in cattle cars with no ventilation except what might slip through a crack in the wood. There were no sanitary facilities. Some died on the terrible journey. The smell of human waste and death was almost unbearable.

The trains were hot, and they rocked violently in the wind. Anne and her family were jammed in with sixty people. Finally, the train stopped. The half-dead people stumbled out and were beaten by SS men who stood guard along the tracks. Anne Frank and her family had arrived at Auschwitz, twenty-five square miles of gas chambers, **crematoriums**, and horror.

Immediately, the men and women were separated. Those to be gassed at once were selected. Anyone over fifty or under fifteen would be gassed along with the sick and disabled. The others were to be put to work. Otto Frank turned and looked at his wife and daughters for the last time on the night of September 5, 1944. Although Otto Frank was fifty-five, he looked younger. For that reason, he was not killed immediately.

The women chosen for the work chores had to walk to the women's camp at Birkenau. Edith Frank and her two daughters stayed together. In October 1944 Edith Frank stayed at Birkenau. But Anne and Margot were sent to the concentration camp at Bergen-Belsen. It was bitterly cold. The women there were starving and getting sick with deadly diseases.

C H A P T E R 10

Anne and Margot huddled together in an icy-cold, unheated **barracks**. Someone who recognized them said the girls looked like frozen little birds. A school friend of Anne's spoke to her once. Anne wept because she believed that both of her parents were dead. Anne was trembling. She was wrapped in one thin blanket.

Typhus swept through Bergen-Belsen in the spring of 1945. Witnesses told of seeing both Anne and Margot Frank deathly sick from the disease. The guards had cut off water to the camp. This made sanitation impossible.

A witness found Anne and Margot lying side by side on the same cot. She encouraged the girls to get help. But Anne said that at least they were together and would die in peace with each other.

In March, Margot fell to the floor while trying to rise from her bunk. She died of shock. A few days, later Anne Frank died as well. The bodies of the girls were taken to the mass graves at the camp and buried.

Three weeks later, in April 1945, British troops liberated Bergen-Belsen. Of the eight people who hid in the secret annex, all but Otto Frank died. Of the helpers, Victor Kugler and Johannes Kleiman were imprisoned, but they survived.

On the day when the annex was betrayed, Miep found Anne's diary. She gathered it up along with the loose pages Anne had written on. Miep hoped at the time that she could give them back to Anne when she was liberated.

On January 27, 1945, when the Russian army liberated Auschwitz, Otto Frank was still alive. He heard that his wife was dead. He had no idea what happened to Anne and Margot. Otto Frank moved in with Miep and Jan Gies. He began an agonizing search for his daughters.

Two months later, Otto Frank learned that Anne and Margot had died at Bergen-Belsen. Immediately, Miep gave him the diaries she had saved from the secret annex. Otto Frank was amazed that his daughter had written so much. He was also touched by the quality of the writing.

He shared the diaries with others. They encouraged him to have the work published. In April 1946 Anne Frank's diary was first published. Anne's dream of becoming a writer had come true.

In the years that followed, Anne Frank's diary was published all over the world. It was translated into many languages. Millions of copies were sold. Plays and films based on the life of Anne Frank have been performed throughout the world.

Millions of Jews and other innocent people were murdered by Adolf Hitler and the Nazis. A tragedy so enormous is hard for people to **comprehend**. But, everyone who read the diary of Anne Frank could identify with a beautiful, bright-eyed little girl full of love and hope. Anne Frank's suffering and death brought home to millions of people the horror of prejudice gone mad.

Otto Frank spent the rest of his life spreading the ideals of his daughter. In her diary, she never talked about hating anybody. She hoped her life could be spent making the world a better place. Frank considered it his duty to fulfill his daughter's dreams.

Anne Frank has become a symbol of anyone who is persecuted because of their race, color, or creed anywhere in the world. Visitors today can go to 263 Prinsengracht to view the secret annex and original pages of Anne Frank's diaries. Each year, over 600,000 people come to the Anne Frank house in Amsterdam.

Although Anne Frank lived for just fifteen years and some nine months, she has had a great impact on the world. Her spirit and courage is a **reproach** to anyone who would promote bigotry or hatred.

BIBLIOGRAPHY

Frank, Anne. *Tales From the Secret Annex.* London: Penguin, 1982.

Lee, Carol Anne. *The Hidden Life of Otto Frank.* New York: Harper Collins, 2002.

van der Rol, Rudd and Rian Verhoeven. *Anne Frank: Beyond the Diary.* New York: Viking, 1993.

GLOSSARY

annex: an addition to a building

anti-semitism: prejudice against Jewish people

barracks: a large building in which many people are housed

betray: to give information to someone's enemy

black market: a place where things are bought and sold illegally

boycott: to stop buying or using something in protest

chancellor: the chief political leader of a country

civilian: non-military

comprehend: understand

concentration camps: a place where people are imprisoned and often tortured and killed

confide: to tell ones secrets to someone else

crematorium: a place where bodies are incinerated

criticize: to find fault in

depression: a time of economic problems and decline

extermination camp: a place where people are killed

garments: clothing

gratitude: thankfulness; gratefulness

harassment: the act of bothering or tormenting someone else

hash: a kind of food that includes chopped meat and vegetables

inflation: an increase in the prices of products or a decline in the value of money

mischief: behavior that caused slight annoyance

occupation: the controlling of a foreign territory with military forces

ominous: threatening; warning; worrying

persecution: mistreatment of someone because of his or her religion or beliefs

ration: a fixed amount of food or provisions

refugee: a person who leaves an area to find safety

reproach: to find fault with; blame

Sabbath: Saturday, the seventh day of the week, as the day of rest and religious ceremony among Jews and some Christians

satchel: a shoulder bag or purse

stubborn: difficult to manage; strong-minded

synagogue: a Jewish house of worship

Typhus: a disease passed by lice and fleas

INDEX